W9-CDM-710

EXAMINING ISSUES THROUGH POLITICAL CARTOONS

Civil Liberties and War

Titles in the Examining Issues Through Political Cartoons series include:

Examining Issues Through POLITICAL CARTOONS

Civil Liberties and War

Edited by Andrea C. Nakaya

Bruce Glassman, *Vice President*
Bonnie Szumski, *Publisher*
Helen Cothran, *Managing Editor*
Scott Barbour, *Series Editor*

GREENHAVEN PRESS
An imprint of Thomson Gale, a part of The Thomson Corporation

THOMSON
GALE

Detroit • New York • San Francisco • San Diego • New Haven, Conn.
Waterville, Maine • London • Munich

© 2006 Thomson Gale, a part of The Thomson Corporation.

Thomson and Star Logo are trademarks and Gale and Greenhaven Press are registered trademarks used herein under license.

For more information, contact
Greenhaven Press
27500 Drake Rd.
Farmington Hills, MI 48331-3535
Or you can visit our Internet site at http://www.gale.com

ALL RIGHTS RESERVED.
No part of this work covered by the copyright hereon may be reproduced or used in any form or by any means—graphic, electronic, or mechanical, including photocopying, recording, taping, Web distribution or information storage retrieval systems—without the written permission of the publisher.

Every effort has been made to trace the owners of copyrighted material.

Cover credit: Gorrell. © 2002 by Creators Syndicate, Inc. Reproduced by permission.

LIBRARY OF CONGRESS CATALOGING-IN-PUBLICATION DATA

Civil liberties and war / Andrea C. Nakaya, book editor.
    p. cm. — (Examining issues through political cartoons)
    Includes bibliographical references and index.
    ISBN 0-7377-2517-6 (lib. : alk. paper)
    1. Civil rights—United States—History. 2. Human rights—United States—History. 3. United States—Military policy—Public opinion. 4. War—Public opinion. 5. Public opinion—United States. I. Nakaya, Andrea C., 1976– II. Series.
    JC599.U5C5465 2006
    323'.0973—dc22
                                                             2005050205

Printed in the United States of America

Contents

Foreword

Political cartoons, also called editorial cartoons, are drawings that do what editorials do with words—express an opinion about a newsworthy event or person. They typically appear in the opinion pages of newspapers, sometimes in support of that day's written editorial, but more often making their own comment on the day's events. Political cartoons first gained widespread popularity in Great Britain and the United States in the 1800s when engravings and other drawings skewering political figures were fashionable in illustrated newspapers and comic magazines. By the beginning of the 1900s, editorial cartoons were an established feature of daily newspapers. Today, they can be found throughout the globe in newspapers, magazines, and online publications and the Internet.

Art Wood, both a cartoonist and a collector of cartoons, writes in his book *Great Cartoonists and Their Art*:

> Day in and day out the cartoonist mirrors history; he reduces complex facts into understandable and artistic terminology. He is a political commentator and at the same time an artist.

The distillation of ideas into images is what makes political cartoons a valuable resource for studying social and historical topics. Editorial cartoons have a point to express. Analyzing them involves determining both what the cartoon's point is and how it was made.

Sometimes, the point made by the cartoon may be one that the reader disagrees with, or considers offensive. Such cartoons expose readers to new ideas and thereby challenge them to analyze and question their own opinions and assumptions. In some extreme cases, cartoons provide vivid examples of the thoughts that lie behind heinous acts; for example, the cartoons created by the Nazis illustrate the anti-Semitism that led to the mass persecution of Jews.

Examining controversial ideas is but one way the study of political cartoons can enhance and develop critical thinking skills. Another aspect to cartoons is that they can use symbols to make their point quickly. For example, in a cartoon in *Euthanasia*, Chuck Asay depicts supporters of a legal "right to die" by assisted suicide as vultures. Vultures are birds that eat dead and dying animals and are often a symbol of repulsive and cowardly predators who take advantage of those who have met misfortune or are vulnerable. The reader can infer that Asay is expressing his opposition to physician-assisted suicide by suggesting that its supporters are just as loathsome as vultures. Asay thus makes his point through a quick symbolic association.

An important part of critical thinking is examining ideas and arguments in their historical context. Political cartoonists (reasonably) assume that the typical reader of a newspaper's editorial page already has a basic knowledge of current issues and newsworthy people. Understanding and appreciating political cartoons often requires such knowledge, as well as a familiarity with common icons and symbolic figures (such as Uncle Sam's representing the United States). The need for contextual information becomes especially apparent in historical cartoons. For example, although most people know who Adolf Hitler is, a lack of familiarity with other German political figures of the 1930s may create difficulty in fully understanding cartoons about Nazi Germany made in that era.

Providing such contextual information is one important way that Greenhaven's Examining Issues Through Political Cartoons series seeks to make this unique and revealing resource conveniently accessible to students. Each volume presents a representative and diverse collection of political cartoons focusing on a particular current or historical topic. An introductory essay provides a general overview of the subject matter. Each cartoon is then presented with accompanying information including facts about the cartoonist and information and commentary on the cartoon itself. Finally, each volume contains additional informational resources, including listings of books, articles, and websites; an index; and (for historical topics) a chronology of events. Taken together, the contents of each anthology constitute an amusing and informative resource for students of historical and social topics.

Introduction

In 1942 110,000 U.S. residents were forced from their homes in the western United States. With only two weeks notice, they were required to pack only what they could carry with them. Farms, houses, furniture, and animals were hurriedly sold, given away, or simply left behind as these people were transported to remote areas of the country's interior. In places such as Manzanar, California, and Topaz, Utah, they were incarcerated in camps surrounded by barbed wire fences, guard towers, and armed military guards. These 110,000 people—70,000 of them American citizens—were regarded as potentially disloyal to the United States and were imprisoned in the name of national security. They were denied fundamental civil liberties, but not as a result of any proof that any of them were spies or had planned or committed any acts of sabotage. They were imprisoned because of one thing: their ancestry. They were all Japanese and the United States was at war with Japan.

All governments exert some control over the lives of their citizens. In most cases, though, there are limits on that control. For example, the government cannot usually lock up thousands of people without any proof of wrongdoing. Civil liberties are one form of limitation on the power of a government over its citizens. They guarantee people the freedom to think and act as they choose without government interference, and they protect them from imprisonment without due process of law. However, as the Japanese internment illustrates, during times of war the government sometimes restricts civil liberties that are usually taken for granted. The internment is not an isolated incident. An examination of U.S. history reveals that large numbers of people typically have difficulty exercising their civil liberties during wartime. Accompanying the curtailment of liberties is heated debate over whether these restrictions are necessary or desirable in a free country. Some people argue that citizens are entitled to civil liberties protections at all times, even during war. Others contend that in times of war, civil liberties should be balanced against the need to ensure national security.

Civil Liberties

Many countries have constitutions or similar documents that protect the civil liberties of their citizens. England's constitution, while not a single document, secures the basic rights that are deemed inviolable under natural law. In addition, Great Britain and the majority of European countries are signatories to the European Convention on Human Rights. This 1950 document was created to protect human rights and fundamental freedoms such as the freedom of expression, the freedom of association, and the right to a fair trial. In Canada numerous civil liberties are delineated in the Canadian Charter of Rights and Freedoms, including freedom of the press, freedom of expression, and freedom of religion.

Civil liberties protections in the United States date back to the country's origins in 1776. America's founding fathers believed that freedom was their natural right, and when they created the Constitution one of their goals was to protect that right. As author Paul L. Murphy explains, "The Americans of 1776 were convinced that liberty . . . was not only central, but was their birthright. Further, the key to that liberty was personal independence—the ability of individuals to control their own destinies on their own terms."[1] These early Americans believed that a democratic government must allow its citizens to participate and speak without fear of persecution and political repression. Civil liberties guarantees allowed even unpopular points of view to be expressed. They were seen as essential to preventing the emergence of a tyrannical government such as the British monarchy against which the colonists had so recently rebelled.

These guarantees were written into the Constitution and the Bill of Rights. The Constitution is the legal document that assigns and distributes government powers, and it contains both explicit and implicit limits on government powers. However, when the Constitution was submitted to the original thirteen states for approval, many felt it did not contain sufficient civil liberties protections.

More limits on government power were thus added in the form of constitutional amendments. The first ten amendments, also known as the Bill of Rights, contain the majority of civil liberties protections. The best known is the First Amendment, which protects the freedoms of speech, press, religion, and assembly. Other civil liberties contained in the Bill of Rights include the right to bear arms, the right to due process of law, the right to a fair, speedy jury trial, and protection from unreasonable searches, arrests, and seizures of property.

Although these guarantees may seem straightforward, when they are applied to everyday situations they often become more difficult to interpret. For example, the First Amendment states, "Congress shall make no law . . . abridging the freedom of speech." But this leads to questions such as "How should 'speech' be defined?" and "Can symbolic actions such as flag burning be considered a form of speech?" and "What about speech that is harmful to others, such as obscenity or hate speech?" It is the responsibility of the U.S. Supreme Court to interpret and define the Constitution in order to answer questions such as these when they arise. Thus, the definition of civil liberties is based on a combination of constitutional mandates and Supreme Court decisions, and it continues to evolve over time.

Civil Liberties and War

While the United States and its Constitution in theory provide broad protection of civil liberties, in reality that protection has varied over time. Specifically, the historical record shows that attitudes about civil liberties often change when the nation is engaged in a war. Under war conditions the government frequently restricts civil liberties and is usually supported in its actions by the Supreme Court and the majority of the population. When faced with a threatening enemy, Americans tend to unite in order to fight that enemy, and national security becomes the dominant concern. In this united effort to ensure security, there is often little tolerance for individuals and groups that challenge government policies or the status quo. Civil liberties restrictions such as surveillance or suppression of dissent, while unacceptable during times of peace, are frequently viewed as acceptable ways to protect the country during a war. For example, in 1942 when thousands of Japanese were incarcerated in internment camps, a poll showed that only 31 percent of Americans favored allowing them to return to their homes. The majority was afraid that if freed, the Japanese would engage in sabotage against the United States. In the face of this threat, they preferred to restrict the civil liberties of the minority in an attempt to ensure safety for the majority.

Are Restrictions Ever Justified?

Many civil libertarians argue that the restriction of civil liberties during war is unconstitutional. They believe that the Constitution guarantees certain rights and that these rights are absolute, even in times of war. Former superior court judge Andrew P. Napolitano maintains, "It is only a warped view of American history, culture, and law that could seriously suggest that constitutional rights are discretionary." He discusses the danger of interpreting the Constitution according to the wants and needs of the government. In his opinion, this practice will lead to a country in which the government has the power to unfairly violate the rights of its citizens—a country where "we will continue to see public trials in some cities and secret trials in others; free speech suppressed on inexplicable whims; police targeting the weak and killing the innocent; and government lying to its citizens, stealing their property, and tricking them into criminal acts . . . and breaking the laws in order to enforce them."[2] Constitutionally mandated civil liberties protect citizens from government abuse, says Napolitano, and if the government has the power to change these constitutional protections at will, they become meaningless. The late Supreme Court justice Thurgood Marshall warned that during times of crisis, not only should civil liberties be preserved, but they should be fiercely guarded. "History teaches us that grave threats to liberty often come in times of urgency," he says, "when constitutional rights seem too extravagant to endure."[3]

Further, argue civil liberties advocates, the effects of civil liberties restrictions during war are frequently long lasting. These critics argue that war is often used as an excuse for unnecessary restrictions that may last for years after the conflict has subsided. Author Michael Linfield maintains that civil liberties restrictions in the United States do not end with the signing of a peace treaty. "For the period often lasting as long as ten to fifteen years before and after each war, the civil liberties of U.S. citizens have been trampled

11

underfoot as if the Constitution did not exist,"[4] he says. Writer Clair Wilcox commented on this trend during the Cold War between America and the Soviet Union. "We Americans are having the jitters again," she said. "We have had them before and we have got over them. We shall doubtless survive the present attack as well. But the seizure, while it lasts, is painful. It may drag on for years. And it is certain to leave its scar upon us." According to Wilcox, every wartime restriction of civil liberties forces Americans to fight anew to regain these rights. She says, "When the going is hard, we permit [constitutional] values to be lost from sight. In every generation, we must discover them anew."[5]

Many people disagree with this position, however, contending that while civil liberties are important, they must continually be balanced with other concerns, such as security. Supreme Court chief justice William H. Rehnquist explains that while Americans do have civil liberties, this does not mean that they are free from all government restraint. Rehnquist examines the words "civil liberty" and points out that the word "civil" is derived from "citizen" and that a citizen is a person owing allegiance to some government. In his opinion personal liberties such as freedom of speech must be balanced with the liberties of other individuals and the government. He explains that if there was no check on freedom, then the majority would lose their freedom. "In any civilized society the most important task is achieving a proper balance between freedom and order," he maintains. "It simply cannot be said . . . that in every conflict between individual liberty and governmental authority the former should prevail."[6] Lawyer Richard A. Posner echoes Rehnquist. He argues that to most effectively protect the citizens of a country, the law—including the Constitution—must be malleable. "[The law] is an instrument for promoting social welfare, and as the conditions essential to that welfare change, so must it change,"[7] he maintains.

Rehnquist, Posner, and others believe that in accordance with this idea of balance, the emphasis on civil liberties must change in times of war. They argue that during war, civil liberties must be reevaluated in relation to threats the country faces and should be curtailed to the extent that the benefits of greater security outweigh the costs in reduced liberty. According to Rehnquist, "It is neither desirable nor is it remotely likely that civil liberty will occupy as favored a position in wartime as it does in peacetime." He argues that "the laws will . . . not be silent in time of war, but they will speak with a somewhat different voice."[8] Proponents of this position maintain that civil liberties can be restored when the danger is passed. They emphasize that while officials might overestimate the threat to security—for example the threat of Japanese Americans during World War II—these excesses can only be seen in hindsight. Thus, in order to protect the country, the government should err on the side of caution, even if some restrictions are later revealed to be unnecessary. Some people argue, for example, that the September 11, 2001, terrorist attacks may have been prevented if the government had been more willing to restrict civil liberties to promote security.

Civil Liberties and War in Early American History

America's historical record shows that civil liberties protections are repeatedly rebalanced according to security concerns. Every time the country engages in a war, civil liberties are restricted in the name of national security. Whether or not this restriction is justified remains the topic of continued debate.

Wartime restrictions are rooted in the beginning of U.S. history, starting with the Revolutionary War. Between 1775 and 1783 the American colonies fought for independence from Great Britain, and during that time people's tribunals, loyalty oaths, expropriation of property, and press censorship were all widespread. At the beginning of the war much of the American population was still loyal to the king of England and was opposed to the revolutionaries who were fighting for independence. In an attempt to encourage support for their cause, the revolutionaries created Committees of Safety in numerous towns. These committees identified antirevolutionary sentiment, surveilled Loyalists, and administered loyalty oaths. The Committee of Safety in New York ordered that the weapons of anyone not swearing allegiance to the Revolution be seized. Under a 1776 committee act in Massachusetts, ministers and schoolmasters were to lose their salaries if they did not swear allegiance to the Revolution. Revolutionaries also seized the property of many people loyal to the British Crown. In 1778, for example, Georgia confiscated all property of British subjects. Four years later, 274 Loyalists were banished from the state on pain of death and had their property confiscated. The press was also subject to heavy censorship during the Revolutionary War. In 1775, for example, Massachusetts passed a law stating, "The printers of the newspapers in Boston be ordered upon their peril not to insert in their prints anything of the public affairs of this province relative to the war without the order of the government."[9]

Almost eighty years later America became embroiled in the Civil War, and civil liberties were again suspended. Between 1861 and 1865 President Abraham Lincoln fought to preserve the Union, and he imposed many harsh restrictions in his efforts to accomplish this goal, including press censorship, expropriation of property, and the suspension of habeas corpus. According to Linfield, "During the Civil War, the Constitution was put into a deep freeze."[10] Lincoln seized telegraph lines and established censorship over all transmissions. In addition, newspapers that printed articles unfavorable to the Union were seized or prevented from publishing. For example, in Missouri the *Boone County Standard* was accused of encouraging resistance to the war. Its editor was subsequently banished from the state, and the presses were seized and sold for the benefit of the army. The most notorious restriction of civil liberties during the Civil War was Lincoln's suspension of habeas corpus, which, according to the Constitution, may only be suspended by Congress. Habeas corpus allows prisoners to request to be brought before a judge to determine whether their imprisonment is justified. Lincoln believed that this process was too slow and difficult, so between ten thousand and thirty thousand people were arrested during the war and denied the benefit of habeas corpus hearings. Lincoln justified his actions as essential to national security. He argued that by breaking one law he could preserve others. "Are all the laws but one to go unexecuted," he asked, "and the government itself go to pieces lest that one be violated?"[11] When the suspension was challenged in court, Chief Justice Roger B. Taney found that Lincoln had violated the Constitution. Lincoln ignored him and was supported by the majority of the press and the public, who criticized Taney's decision.

Civil Liberties in the Twentieth Century

When America entered World War I in 1917, the president again faced widespread public opposition to government policies. To combat public disapproval of America's involvement in the war, the government took numerous actions to suppress dissent. In his 1915

State of the Union Address, President Woodrow Wilson argued that dissenters threatened the security of the United States. "There are citizens of the United States . . . who have poured the poison of disloyalty into the very arteries of our national life. . . . Such creatures of passion, disloyalty, and anarchy must be crushed,"[12] he said. The 1917 Espionage Act gave the government the power to punish these dissenters. The act prohibited the transmission of information harmful to national security. It also allowed the imposition of penalties for antiwar commentary and opinions. Amended the next year as the Sedition Act, it gave the government even more power to punish dissenters, who could be sentenced to twenty years in jail and/or a ten-thousand-dollar fine.

Local citizens were also strongly encouraged to enforce patriotism during World War I. For example, in Nevada local citizens held a "people's trial" in which they tarred and feathered a resident guilty of "lukewarmness toward the cause of the United States and their allies."[13] In South Dakota people who did not purchase enough Liberty Bonds to finance the war effort were referred to as slackers and were often subpoenaed and interrogated. The American Protective League was also created to discourage dissent. This privately run patriotic association surveilled and intimidated people whose loyalty it questioned. During this time the government frequently looked the other way at incidents of violence committed against "disloyal" citizens, reasoning that dissenters were harmful to national security. After the lynching of a German miner, for example, one senator stated, "Of course, I would rather not have mob law, but if we can't take care of them any other way, popular justice will do it."[14]

There was also widespread media censorship during World War I. To facilitate this undertaking, the Committee on Public Information (CPI) was created in 1917. As the official U.S. censorship board, the CPI helped present a government-approved message about the war and used censorship to exclude other opinions. The CPI justified this censorship with the argument that Congress had the right to restrict freedom of the press during wartime if such actions were necessary to national security. The committee stated:

> Congress may establish a censorship of the press in war time if circumstances render such a measure "necessary and proper" . . . and the subjugation of the press to the powers

given Congress by the Constitution can hardly be said to *abridge* . . . freedom. Also, of course, Congress may penalize publications which are calculated to stir up sedition, to obstruct the carrying out of the laws, or to "give aid and comfort to the enemy" (which is treason). Freedom of the press in war time rests, therefore, largely with the discretion of Congress.[15]

In 1941 America entered another world war and civil liberties were again heavily restricted. During World War II the Federal Bureau of Investigation was given authority to censor all news and control all communications going into and out of the country. In addition, the Office of Censorship was created to censor news and enforce a code of wartime restrictions for press and radio. At the U.S. Post Office, censors cut articles out of the *Los Angeles Times* with razor blades before sending the newspaper to subscribers overseas. Battle news was heavily censored in order to preserve morale. For example, a 1942 U.S. loss at Savo Island in the Pacific Ocean was not announced until nine weeks after the event. World War II was the first time in U.S. history that a passport was required to leave the country, and many people were denied passports if the government believed their travel would be prejudicial to the interests of the United States.

Japanese Americans experienced some of the greatest civil liberties restrictions during the war. In response to the 1941 attack on Pearl Harbor, President Franklin Delano Roosevelt issued Executive Order 9066. Under this order, approximately 110,000 Japanese Americans were placed in internment camps. The average internee spent nine hundred days behind barbed wire. In the camps, reading material was censored and inmates were tested for loyalty. Even those determined to be loyal and released were forced to obtain official approval of their homes, jobs, and friends. A number of Japanese Americans protested the internment and were put in psychiatric hospitals for the remainder of the war. The majority of the American population supported this harsh treatment as essential to national security. General John L. DeWitt, one of those who supported the internment, summed up popular opinion in his testimony before the Senate. According to him, "A Jap's a Jap. . . . There is no way to determine their loyalty. . . . It makes no difference whether he is an

16

American; theoretically he is still a Japanese and you just can't change that."[16] In 1983, however, the government officially recognized that the civil liberties of Japanese Americans had been unfairly violated by these actions. That year, the Congressional Commission on Wartime Relocation unanimously concluded, "Executive Order 9066 was not justified by military necessity." Instead, the committee found, the order was caused by "race prejudice, war hysteria and a failure of political leadership."[17]

Following World War II the United States engaged in another hysterical restriction of civil liberties. A period of rivalry with the Soviet Union and its allies, known as the Cold War, began in the late 1940s. During this time there was intense fear of communism in the United States, and many actions were taken to find Communists and suppress the spread of Communist ideas. Communist organizations were required to register with the attorney general, and their members were subject to numerous restrictions, including limits on the right to travel, the use of mail, and on employment. Even those simply suspected of being Communists or sympathizing with Communists faced great civil liberties restrictions. Large numbers of people were accused of disloyalty and subjected to loyalty hearings where they were questioned about their political and social beliefs. The most famous of these hearings were conducted by Senator Joseph McCarthy. In the McCarthy hearings many government employees and officials were accused of disloyalty to the United States. Many people lost jobs, careers, and reputations as a result of wild, unsubstantiated accusations. According to author Jerel A. Rosati, "The anticommunist hysteria . . . became so intense, and the demands of national security overwhelmed the demands of democracy so thoroughly, that even defending the constitutional rights and liberties of Americans was considered evidence of disloyalty."[18] Fearful of the government's power to take away their jobs and their reputations, millions of Americans gave up their right to free speech and became silent.

During the Vietnam War many opponents of government policies were not so quiet. As this war—the longest in U.S. history—stretched on, opposition to it grew, and an increasing number of Americans engaged in antiwar protests. In response, the government frequently sent federal troops to break up these demonstrations, often with violent results. One of the most notorious was the demonstration at Kent State University in Ohio. On May 4, 1970, the National Guard opened fire on protesters, killing four and wounding many others. Again in 1970, at a demonstration in Jackson, Mississippi, the National Guard opened fire on protesters, killing two students. Incidents such as these often generated little public opposition. A *Newsweek* poll following the Kent State shootings found that 58 percent of the country believed that the students had provoked the guards' fire. During the war, the government also provoked widespread protest by instituting the military draft. Many people believed the government had no right to force them to fight in the war, and hundreds of young men burned their draft cards in protest or fled to countries such as Canada. In response, the government issued thousands of prison sentences for draft resistance or refusal.

The War on Terrorism

In 2001 the United States entered a war unlike any other in its history. In response to the September 11 terrorist attacks that resulted in the deaths of almost three thousand people, it embarked on a war against terrorism. Once again, as America fights to protect itself from enemies—this time terrorists—civil liberties restrictions have been enacted. The most controversial of these is the Patriot Act, enacted in 2001. The act expanded the government's information-sharing and surveillance capacities, changed criminal justice procedures, and imposed new immigration restrictions. Other controversial restrictions in the war on terror are the use of racial profiling and the detention of suspected terrorists without due process.

The debates over these new civil liberties restrictions mirror past wartime debates, with extensive disagreement over the relative importance of civil liberties and national security. Supporters of the Patriot Act and other restrictions argue that if America wants to prevent another devastating terrorist attack like September 11, it must curtail some civil liberties. Author Amitai Etzioni argues that it would be wrong to try to preserve civil liberties at the expense of security. He says, "It's a mistake to think of homeland security as a zero sum game, where 100 percent of the turf belongs to rights, and every new safety measure amounts to an intrusion to be justified. To realize how prejudicial this approach is, ask the opposite, equally loaded question: How far should we be willing to sacrifice our security in order to enhance our rights?" In Etzioni's opinion, the definition of reasonable and unreasonable restrictions on civil liberties has changed in light of the deaths that occurred on September 11. In his opinion, the threat of terrorism means that many limits on liberties are now reasonable because they are the best way to prevent another attack. "Much of what was unreasonable before 9/11 ceased to be so that morning,"[19] he says. Former U.S. attorney general John Ashcroft also reasons that if civil liberties are not balanced with national security, America may experience another attack. He criticizes those people who focus on liberty above all else, arguing that Americans must temporarily suppress their dissent and unite to defeat terrorism. "To those who scare peace-loving people with phantoms of lost liberty," says Ashcroft, "my message is this: Your tactics only aid terrorists—for they erode our national unity and diminish our resolve. They give ammunition to America's enemies."[20]

However, civil liberties advocates charge that civil liberties are seriously and unnecessarily threatened by America's war on terror. According to Congressman John Conyers, "[Congress] legislated in hysteria in October of 2001," something "[it has] done before in times of crisis."[21] Human rights advocate David Cole agrees. "With the exception of the right to bear arms," he says, "one would be hard pressed to name a single constitutional liberty that the Bush Administration has not overridden in the name of protecting our freedom."[22] Conyers, Cole, and others maintain that not only has the curtailment of civil liberties failed to improve national security, but it has also taken away the accountability of the government. They argue that when the government bypasses constitutional civil liberties protections in its hunt for terrorists, American citizens lose their ability to be informed about, and to participate in, their government. According to writer Charles Levendosky, "The Justice Department has erected a one-way mirror between itself and the American people—department officials can look out, but Americans can't look in."[23]

A Slippery Slope

As America's history of civil liberties during wartime suggests, the liberties set forth in the Constitution and the Bill of Rights are far from absolute. For as long as these documents have existed, there has been debate over how far civil liberties protections should extend. This debate has been particularly pronounced when the United States is at war. During these periods the government has taken many actions to curtail the civil liberties of Americans, justifying these actions in the name of national security. In response, civil liberties advocates have warned the public to guard their freedom against government intrusion. There is rarely a place of agreement for these two groups. Political cartoonists frequently address these conflicting viewpoints about civil liberties. *Examining Issues Through Political Cartoons: Civil Liberties and War* presents cartoons that explore numerous facets of this controversial topic. In the first chapter the cartoonists examine civil liberties and war in American history. The remaining chapters offer various perspectives on civil liberties in relation to the war on terrorism and the war in Iraq.

The war on terror has provoked special concern because of the fact that this war has no end in sight. Thus, many people argue, civil liberties restrictions may become permanent. Writer Richard C. Leone warns, "The struggle against terrorism could continue for generations, and we run the risk of finding ourselves on a slippery slope, making decisions in which freedoms that are set aside for the 'emergency' become permanently lost to us."[24]

Notes

1. Paul L. Murphy, "The Bill of Rights in Our Historical Development," in Stephen C. Halpern, ed., *The Future of Our Liberties.* Westport, CT: Greenwood, p. 19.

2. Andrew P. Napolitano, "How the Government Breaks the Law," *CATO Policy Report*, November/December 2004, p. 15.

3. Thurgood Marshall, *Skinner v. Railway Labor Executive*, 1989.

4. Michael Linfield, *Freedom Under Fire: U.S. Civil Liberties in Times of War.* Boston: South End, 1990, p. 2.

5. Clair Wilcox, ed., *Civil Liberties Under Attack.* Philadelphia: University of Pennsylvania Press, 1951, p. 2.

6. William H. Rehnquist, *All the Laws but One.* New York: Alfred A. Knopf, 1998, p. 222.

7. Richard A. Posner, "The Truth About Our Liberties," *Responsive Community*, Summer 2002, p. 6.

8. Rehnquist, *All the Laws but One*, p. 225.

9. Quoted in Linfield, *Freedom Under Fire*, p. 15.

10. Linfield, *Freedom Under Fire*, p. 23.

11. Quoted in Linfield, *Freedom Under Fire*, p. 27.

12. Woodrow Wilson, State of the Union Address, 1915.

13. Quoted in Linfield, *Freedom Under Fire*, p. 37.

14. Quoted in Linfield, *Freedom Under Fire*, p. 40.

15. Quoted in Linfield, *Freedom Under Fire*, p. 49.

16. Quoted in Linfield, *Freedom Under Fire*, p. 96.

17. Quoted in Linfield, *Freedom Under Fire*, p. 96.

18. Jerel A. Rosati, "At Odds with One Another: The Tension Between Civil Liberties and National Security in Twentieth-Century America," in David B. Cohen and John W. Wells, eds., *American National Security and Civil Liberties in an Era of Terrorism*. New York: Palgrave Macmillan, 2004, p. 16.

19. Amitai Etzioni, "Better Safe than Sorry," *Weekly Standard*, July 21, 2003, p. 29.

20. John Ashcroft, testimony before the Senate Judiciary Committee, December 7, 2001.

21. Quoted in Christopher P. Banks, "Protecting (or Destroying) Freedom Through Law: The USA PATRIOT Act's Constitutional Implications," in David B. Cohen and John W. Wells, eds., *American National Security and Civil Liberties in an Era of Terrorism*. New York: Palgrave Macmillan, 2004, p. 30.

22. David Cole, "Enemy Aliens and American Freedoms," *Nation*, September 23, 2002, p. 20.

23. Charles Levendosky, "Patriot Act Chills First Amendment Freedoms," *Liberal Opinion Week*, February 3, 2003, p. 12.

24. Richard C. Leone, "The Quiet Republic: The Missing Debate About Civil Liberties After 9/11," in Richard C. Leone and Greg Anrig Jr., eds., *The War on Our Freedoms: Civil Liberties in an Age of Terrorism*. New York: PublicAffairs, 2003, p. 6.

Chapter 1

Civil Liberties and War in American History

EXAMINING ISSUES THROUGH
POLITICAL CARTOONS

Preface

The First Amendment to the U.S. Constitution states that Congress shall make no law "abridging the freedom of speech or of the press." In 1919, however, American citizen Kate Richards O'Hare was one of hundreds of Americans prosecuted by the government for exercising this right to free speech. O'Hare was sentenced to five years in prison for protesting U.S. involvement in World War I. Prosecutors charged that she had called American women "nothing more or less than brood-sows, to raise children to get into the army and be turned into fertilizer." Under the 1918 Sedition Act, any such expression of "disloyalty" was a crime in the United States. World War I is not the only time that constitutionally guaranteed civil liberties have been suspended in America. The Sedition Act is only one example of the way civil liberties are frequently restricted when the United States is at war.

The Sedition Act outlawed many forms of dissent during World War I. Included in the act's prohibitions was a ban on saying or printing anything "disloyal . . . scurrilous, or abusive" about the government, saying or doing anything that would cause "contempt, scorn . . . or disrepute" of the armed forces, favoring the cause of any country with which the United States was at war, or advocating the curtailment of production of any goods necessary to the war effort. Anyone violating the law could be sentenced to twenty years in jail and/or a fine of ten thousand dollars.

The government and the U.S. Supreme Court defended the Sedition Act on the grounds that it was essential to the U.S. war effort. They believed that censorship of dissent was essential to keeping up the spirit of the U.S. Army and of the American people. They were also afraid that public expression of dissent might encourage Americans to engage in spying, sabotage, or other actions that might prevent America from winning the war. A statement by Supreme Court justice Oliver Wendell Holmes Jr. summed up the attitude at the time. Holmes argued, "When a nation is at war, many things that might be said in time of peace are such a hindrance to its effort that their utterance will not be endured so long as men fight and no Court could regard them as protected by any constitutional right." In addition to keeping up morale and preventing sabotage, lawmakers maintained that the law actually protected dissenters. It was said that if a person expressed disloyalty to the United States they might incur mob violence so great that it would be impossible for the government to protect them.

Opponents of the act protested that it prevented people from expressing their opinions freely as mandated in the Constitution. Civil liberties advocates such as journalist Robert Higgs believe that the constitutional protection of freedom of speech and of the press is absolute, and it is unconstitutional to restrict that freedom, even during war. Higgs points out, "[The Supreme Court decision to uphold the Sedition Act] might strike the proverbial Man from Mars as odd, because the Constitution itself makes no provision for its own evisceration during wartime." Further, as author Michael Linfield argues, while the act was justified as essential to preventing spying and sabotage, America did not need such stringent protections during World War I. "Although the purported rationale for the [act] was to protect the government from enemies and foreign agents," says Linfield, "not a single person was ever convicted of spying [during World War I]."

While it may surprise many people that Americans like Kate Richards O'Hare have received prison sentences merely for voicing their opinions, U.S. history shows that similar civil liberties restrictions have occurred frequently during times of war. In this chapter the cartoonists offer commentary on civil liberties during various U.S. wars. While the Sedition Act was repealed in 1921, an examination of history reveals that in every war that America has experienced there has been some degree of civil liberties restriction.

Examining Cartoon 1:
"The Yankee Guy Fawkes"

PLATE No. 126   The Yankee Guy Fawkes, London Fun, November 7, 1863

About the Cartoon

This Civil War–era cartoon by English cartoonist Matt Morgan refers to Guy Fawkes Day, a popular English holiday celebrating the 1605 failure of an attempt to blow up the English Parliament. Guy Fawkes celebrations involve a fireworks display and the building of a bonfire. On that bonfire, an effigy of Guy Fawkes, the most famous of the plot conspirators, is traditionally burned.

In this cartoon American president Abraham Lincoln is depicted burning an effigy of George Washington—one of America's founding fathers and the country's first president—on a Guy Fawkes bonfire. In the original publication, Lincoln is shouting, "I'll warn yer. Your old Constitution won't do U.S." The effigy inscribed with the words "Charter of American Laws" and "States Rights," seems to represent the American union and its Constitution. Documents labeled "Draft," "Emancipation," and "Suspension," add fuel to the bonfire that is destroying the Union. The cartoonist's use of the Guy Fawkes theme is thus ironic; whereas the British version of Guy Fawkes Day celebrates the survival of the country, the American version, at least as perceived by this British cartoonist, celebrates the nation's destruction.

During the Civil War, Lincoln's aim was to preserve the Union. In this cartoon, however, Morgan suggests that Lincoln's Civil War actions—specifically, mandating a military draft, emancipating the slaves, and suspending habeas corpus—were actually unconstitutional and were destroying the principles upon which the Union was based. According to the Constitution, the president does not have the authority to suspend habeas corpus. Lincoln, however, did so a number of times during the war in order to gain power to punish those disloyal to the Union. The Supreme Court declared Lincoln's actions unconstitutional, but he ignored their decision.

About the Cartoonist

Matt Morgan was an English cartoonist whose Civil War–era cartoons criticizing Lincoln and the Union were regularly published in the *London Fun* newspaper.

Morgan. *London Fun*, 1863.

26

Examining Cartoon 2:
"The Naughty Boy"

THE NAUGHTY BOY GOTHAM, WHO WOULD NOT TAKE THE DRAFT.

About the Cartoon

When the U.S. Civil War began in 1861, the men who fought for the Union were volunteers. Voluntary service, however, did not produce enough soldiers, and in 1863 Congress passed a law authorizing a military draft. According to the law, President Abraham Lincoln could draft into military service "all able-bodied male citizens and all persons of foreign birth who had declared their intentions to become citizens, between the ages of twenty and forty-five."

This 1863 cartoon by an unknown artist depicts the controversy the draft law evoked. Many people protested it as an unconstitutional violation of their civil liberties. Through the unhappy expressions of both children in the cartoon, the artist portrays the draft as an unpleasant medicine that Lincoln, depicted as the mother, is forcing them to take. The cartoon originally appeared with this plea by Lincoln set beside it: "There now, you bad boy, acting that way, when your little sister Penn takes hers like a baby." While many Americans did express opposition to the draft, they largely ended up accepting it, as shown by the little girl, "Penn," or Philadelphia, who has quietly taken her medicine. However, there was violent opposition to the draft in some places. In New York, represented here by Gotham throwing a tantrum, draft riots caused widespread destruction of property and the deaths or injuries of more than one thousand people.

Unknown. *Frank Leslie's Illustrated Newspaper*, 1863.

Examining Cartoon 3:

"So Long As Men Can Do THIS They're FREE!"

About the Cartoon

One important civil liberty protected in the United States and many other countries is the right to dissent, even against the government during wartime. In this World War II cartoon Theodor

Geisel celebrates that right. The cartoon shows a crowd of men thumbing their noses at Adolf Hitler, leader of Nazi Germany during the war. One of the men carries a banner proclaiming, "So long as men can do THIS they're FREE!" Even the bird atop the pole thumbs his nose at Hitler. In contrast to this ideal of free speech, Hitler harshly suppressed all dissent against him, killing millions of his opponents during the war.

At the time this cartoon was published Hitler had not yet been defeated by the Allies. However, Geisel implies that regardless of whether they are winning or losing the war, the Allies will triumph because they possess the power of freedom. A wide-eyed, disheveled-looking Hitler in the background and the sticks carried by the men rushing toward him imply that Hitler will be defeated because freedom is more powerful than suppression.

About the Cartoonist

Theodor Geisel, better known as "Dr. Seuss," is the author of numerous political cartoons commenting on the events of World War II. He is also the author of many well-known children's books. He died in 1991.

Theodor Seuss Geisel, illustrator. From an illustration in *Dr. Seuss Goes to War: The World War II Editorial Cartoons of Theodor Seuss Geisel*, by Richard H. Minear. New York: The New Press, 1999. Illustration Copyright © 1942 by *Marshall Field, the Newspaper PM*. Text and compilation copyright © 1999 by Richard H. Minear. All rights reserved. Reproduced by permission of the publisher.

Examining Cartoon 4:
"A Jap Is a Jap"

About the Cartoon

In 1941 the Japanese bombed Pearl Harbor, Hawaii, and in response the United States declared war on Japan. The surprise Pearl Harbor attack led many Americans to suspect that the Japanese were preparing a full-scale attack on the West Coast, and military officials and civilians began to question the loyalty of the ethnic Japanese living in that area. As a result, the Japanese were subject to severe restrictions and discrimination as portrayed in this drawing by Mine Okubo. The drawing depicts the author reading a newspaper from San Francisco, her hometown at the time. Around her are some of the stereotypes and accusations that many Japanese were subject to during the war, including, "Don't Trust a Jap" and "We Don't Want Japs." Okubo shows how overwhelming and inescapable these accusations were for many Japanese people.

In 1942 President Franklin D. Roosevelt signed Executive Order 9066, which led to the incarceration of approximately 110,000 Japanese residents from the West Coast and Hawaii, 70,000 of whom were U.S. citizens. This internment is widely regarded as one of the worst civil liberties violations in U.S. history. The average internee was forced to leave behind most of his or her possessions, spend nine hundred days behind barbed wire, and endure censorship and loyalty tests in the camps. Yet during the war, no evidence was found of a single act of spying or sabotage by a Japanese living in America. In 1983 a congressional commission unanimously concluded that "Executive Order 9066 was not justified by military necessity." Instead, the commission found, it was caused by "race prejudice, war hysteria and a failure of political leadership."

About the Cartoonist

Mine Okubo was born in California in 1912 to immigrant Japanese parents. After the bombing of Pearl Harbor, Okubo and her youngest brother were incarcerated in the Topaz internment camp in Utah. They were separated from the rest of their family, who were interned in Montana and Wyoming. Okubo is the author of *Citizen 13660*, a first-person account of the time she spent in the internment camp.

Okubo. © 1964 by Mine Okubo. Reproduced by permission.

Examining Cartoon 5:
"Our Case Couldn't Be Reversed"

"THE DIFFERENCE IS, OUR CASE COULDN'T BE REVERSED"

About the Cartoon

During the Cold War between the United States and the Soviet Union, America experienced intense anticommunism and fear of Communist subversion. In the early 1950s Senator Joseph McCarthy led the McCarthy hearings, a hunt for Communist activity among U.S. government officials. The trials featured unsubstantiated accusations and convictions that tarnished the reputations of many people. McCarthy's efforts to root out Communists are sometimes called a witch hunt, in reference to the Salem witch hunts of 1692, in which a large number of people were falsely accused and executed for witchcraft.

In this cartoon Daniel Robert Fitzpatrick attempts to show how much like the Salem witch hunts the McCarthy hearings really were. The cartoon shows a man who appears to be a judge from the Salem trials. He is speaking with another man who represents the U.S. security system. This man reviews documents while the Salem judge points out, "The difference is, our case couldn't be reversed." By comparing the McCarthy hearings with the Salem trials, the cartoonist suggests that they are a serious violation of civil liberties. The judge states that the McCarthy hearings differ from the Salem trials because the accused have not been executed and the verdict can be reversed. However, Fitzpatrick is implying that the effects of the McCarthy trials were actually very much like the effects of the witch trials; while no one died, many lives were irreversibly ruined by these unfounded accusations of Communist activity.

About the Cartoonist

Daniel Robert Fitzpatrick worked as a cartoonist for the *Chicago Daily News* and the *St. Louis Post-Dispatch*. According to Fitzpatrick, the main purpose of his art was to express "sympathy for the underdog." He twice won the Pulitzer Prize for his cartoons. He died in 1969.

Fitzpatrick. *St. Louis Post-Dispatch*, 1955.

Examining Cartoon 6:
"The U.S. Army Is Watching You"

About the Cartoon

In the latter part of the Vietnam War, many Americans expressed fierce opposition to their country's involvement in the Southeast Asian nation. In numerous cases, government troops were sent to suppress antiwar demonstrators, sometimes resulting in the injury or even the death of protesters.

In this cartoon, Paul Conrad has altered a popular U.S. Army recruitment poster to suggest that in addition to suppressing protesters, the government is also conducting surveillance on antiwar demonstrators. By changing "wants you," to "is watching you" Conrad implies that the U.S. military is no longer concerned with its primary purpose of fighting and recruiting soldiers but is focused instead on observing American students, hippies, and others who are demonstrating against the war.

About the Cartoonist

Three-time Pulitzer Prize–winner Paul Conrad was chief editorial cartoonist for the *Los Angeles Times* from 1964 to 1993. His cartoons appear in newspapers nationwide and abroad and are syndicated five days a week by the Los Angeles Times Syndicate. His books include *CONartist, Drawn and Quartered,* and *When in the Course of Human Events.*

Conrad. © 1970 by Tribune Media Services, Inc. All rights reserved. Reproduced by permission.

Chapter 2

Civil Liberties and America's War on Terrorism

EXAMINING ISSUES THROUGH POLITICAL CARTOONS

Preface

R acial profiling occurs when law enforcement officers question, search, or arrest someone based on their race, ethnicity, or national origin. Before the September 11, 2001, terrorist attacks, polls revealed that the majority of Americans were opposed to this practice because they believed it violated civil liberties. On September 11, 2001, this consensus evaporated. The nineteen al Qaeda terrorists who hijacked airplanes to carry out the attacks on the World Trade Center and the Pentagon were Arabs from Muslim countries. The federal government immediately focused massive investigative resources and law enforcement attention on Arabs, Muslims, and those perceived to be Arab or Muslim.

Post–September 11 polls show that the majority of the U.S. public approved of this singling out of young Arab or Muslim men for questioning and detention. With the fear of another attack still strong, many people were willing to restrict civil liberties in an effort to enhance national security. Today the fear of a terrorist attack has lessened slightly, however racial profiling remains a contentious issue. A fierce debate rages over whether or not the United States should use this practice in its efforts to prevent another terrorist attack. Some people believe that Arab or Muslim men are statistically more likely to be terrorists and must therefore be more closely scrutinized. Others contend that thousands of peaceful Arabs and Muslims reside in the United States and to single them out as suspects simply on the basis of ethnicity is a gross violation of their civil liberties.

Because the September 11 attackers were all Arabs and because the majority of al Qaeda members are also Arabs, a number of people have argued that it is only logical to use racial profiling to thwart future terrorist plots. Columnist Michael Kinsey explains the logic behind the use of racial profiling in airport security. "An Arab man heading toward a plane is statistically more likely to be a terrorist," says Kinsey. "That likelihood is infinitesimal, but the whole airport rigmarole is based on infinitesimal chances. . . . Logic says you should pay more attention to people who look like Arabs than to people who don't. This is true even if you are free of all ethnic prejudices. It's not racism." In Kinsey's opinion, it is absurd not to use racial profiling. "We're at war with a terrorist network that . . . has anonymous agents in our country planning more slaughter," he argues. "Are we really supposed to ignore the one identifiable fact we know about them?"

Some argue that the fear of violating civil liberties through racial profiling may actually kill. In a 2001 *Spectator* article, columnist Mark Steyn cites a number of pre–September 11 occurrences that should have alerted the Federal Bureau of Investigation (FBI) to the coming attack. In 2000, for example, FBI agent Kenneth Williams sent an internal memo advising that an unusual number of terrorist leader Osama bin Laden's supporters had been attending civil aviation universities and colleges in the United States. Steyn believes that by following up on this memo and other related information, the FBI may have had a chance to prevent the September 11 attacks. According to Steyn, however, the agency failed to take action for fear of appearing racist by singling out Arabs. "Thousands of Americans died because of ethnic squeamishness by federal agencies," he concludes.

Civil libertarians contend that civil liberties are important protections that the government cannot take away, even in times of war or crisis. Activist Penn Jillette agrees that the threat of terrorism is a serious concern, but in his opinion so are government actions that threaten freedom. "There's no such thing as an acceptable loss of innocent life," he states, "but, isn't the same thing true for freedom? Isn't any loss of freedom unacceptable?" Nadine Strossen and Timothy Edgar of the American Civil Liberties Union concur. According to them, "racial profiling . . . violates our nation's basic constitutional commitment to equality before the law."

The ACLU is one of many organizations that have cataloged numerous violations experienced as a result of racial profiling. For example, Strossen and Edgar relate the case of "Mr. H.," a Pakistani who has lived in the United States for eighteen years and is the sole provider for his wife and four-year-old son, a U.S. citizen. According to Strossen and Edgar, Mr. H. was arrested in 2001 following the accusations of a coworker. She charged Mr. H., who worked as a nurse, with "behaving suspiciously." Based only on the observation that he was Arab and was wearing his surgical mask "more than necessary," he was detained for six months.

Racial profiling is only one of the ways civil liberties have been restricted in America's war on terrorism. In this chapter the cartoonists present various views on the role of civil liberties as the United States tries to protect itself from another terrorist attack. As these drawings suggest, there are no easy answers to this controversial issue.

Examining Cartoon 1:
"A Time When Fear and Suspicion Gripped the Nation"

TODAY WE'RE RELEASING TRANSCRIPTS FROM A TIME WHEN FEAR AND SUSPICION GRIPPED THE NATION!

McCARTHY HEARINGS

A TIME WHEN MANY THOUGHT COMMUNISTS WERE EVERYWHERE!

ONE HOPES WE CAN LEARN A LESSON FROM THIS PARANOIA! ANY QUESTIONS?

YES,,, THE GUY THAT LOOKS LIKE AN ISLAMIC-ARAB TERRORIST IN THE BACK ROW.

Joe Heller *Green Bay Press-Gazette*

About the Cartoon

In this cartoon Uncle Sam is pictured at a press conference, holding transcripts from the McCarthy hearings, which he describes as a time of "fear and suspicion." The McCarthy hearings took place in the early 1950s, a period of intense anticommunism in the United States. Senator Joseph McCarthy terrorized many people and falsely tarnished numerous reputations with his public investigations and unsubstantiated accusations of Communist activity. He

41

was ultimately censured by the U.S. Senate for his unscrupulous methods of inquiry.

"One hopes we can learn a lesson from this paranoia," states Uncle Sam in the cartoon, implying that America will never again engage in civil liberties violations like those of the McCarthy hearings. However in the next frame, he takes a question from a member of the press that he describes as "the guy that looks like an Islamic-Arab terrorist." Here, cartoonist Joe Heller suggests that in its war on terror, America is engaging in the same paranoia against Arab Americans as it did against suspected Communists during the McCarthy hearings. His implication is that America has in fact failed to learn the lesson of the McCarthy era.

About the Cartoonist

Joe Heller has been the editorial cartoonist for the *Green Bay Press-Gazette* since 1985. He has received numerous awards, including seven Best of Gannett Awards, five Milwaukee Press Club Awards, and two national John Fischetti Editorial Cartoon Awards.

Heller. © 2005 by the *Green Bay Press-Gazette*. Reproduced by permission.

Examining Cartoon 2:
"Protecting Americans from Terror Attacks"

About the Cartoon

The American Civil Liberties Union (ACLU) is one of numerous civil liberties groups that fight to protect the civil liberties of Americans. It is a vocal opponent of any government measures that restrict these liberties, including many of those that are part of the current war on terrorism. In this cartoon Wayne Stayskal criticizes the ACLU for its inflexible belief that civil liberties should never be compromised. He suggests that in its quest to protect civil liberties, the ACLU is actually making America vulnerable to attack.

The cartoon depicts a group of terrorists about to commit an act of terrorism and suggests that if caught, they will appeal to the ACLU for help. Stayskal implies that the ACLU is not balancing civil liberties with national security. He seems to be arguing that the ACLU should relax its stringent protection of civil liberties to allow the government enough power to prevent terrorism.

About the Cartoonist

Wayne Stayskal is editorial cartoonist for the *Tampa Tribune*. He is also nationally syndicated by Tribune Media Services and has illustrated several books.

Stayskal. © 2004 by Tribune Media Services, Inc. All rights reserved. Reproduced by permission.

Examining Cartoon 3:
"Which Parts?"

About the Cartoon

Following the September 11, 2001, terrorist attacks on America Congress passed the Patriot Act. The act allows greater search and surveillance powers for government agencies, purportedly giving them the authority they need to find terrorists and uncover future terrorist plots. As illustrated in this cartoon by John Branch, many people are opposed to the Patriot Act because they believe these expanded powers will lead to abuse. Branch offers a humorous exaggeration of possible Patriot Act abuses by picturing former U.S. attorney general John Ashcroft, a vocal supporter of the act, visiting the home of a man who has criticized the act on his telephone.

The cartoon suggests that the act is allowing the government to conduct unnecessary surveillance on ordinary citizens—surveillance that goes beyond finding and preventing terrorists. Branch also suggests that the government has attempted to suppress any protest about its actions. Ashcroft is shown intimidating and interrogating the man for questioning the scope of the Patriot Act.

About the Cartoonist

John Branch has been editorial cartoonist for the *San Antonio Express-News* in Texas since 1981. His work has been reprinted in the *New York Times*, *USA Today*, *Newsweek*, and numerous college newspapers.

Branch. © 2004 by the *San Antonio Express-News*. Reproduced by permission.

Examining Cartoon 4:
"Wolf! Wolf!!"

About the Cartoon

In response to the September 11, 2001, terrorist attacks Congress passed the Patriot Act. Many people immediately protested that the act would invite civil liberties abuses because it gives the government increased search and surveillance powers and decreases the public's knowledge about such actions. In this cartoon, Gary Brookins suggests that such claims are exaggerated. The Patriot Act is represented by a tiny dog. In addition to appearing harmless, the dog is securely leashed and is in a fenced yard. This depiction implies that the Patriot Act is not a threat and that it will not allow the government to escape accountability to the American public. Brookins shows critics, portrayed as the man with the briefcase who is calling the dog a wolf, as illogically afraid of the act. He is suggesting that critics are greatly overreacting to the Patriot Act and that in reality there is nothing to be afraid of.

About the Cartoonist

Gary Brookins is editorial cartoonist for the *Richmond Times-Dispatch* in Virginia. His cartoons appear in numerous newspapers and periodicals throughout the United States. Brookins is also the recipient of the 1980 George Washington Honor Medal from the Freedom Foundation and a 1979 Dragonslayer Citation from the U.S. Industrial Council.

Brookins. © 2003 by the *Richmond Times-Dispatch*. Reproduced by permission.

Examining Cartoon 5:
"Unless the President Decides He's a Bad Guy"

About the Cartoon

According to the U.S. Constitution, anyone charged with a crime is entitled to due process of law. Since the September 11, 2001, terrorist attacks, however, hundreds of suspected terrorists have been incarcerated indefinitely without access to a lawyer and without being charged with a crime. Many have been imprisoned at a U.S. detention center in Guantánamo Bay, Cuba, where the George W.

Bush administration has classified them as enemy combatants, whom the administration claims are not entitled to constitutional rights. With this cartoon, Ben Sargent criticizes Bush—pictured altering the Constitution—for his treatment of these prisoners. Bush's disregard for the constitutional mandates of due process is depicted as a desecration of this important document. Sargent implies that Bush mistakenly thinks he is not bound by the civil liberties protections that govern all Americans. Rather than following judicial procedures outlined in the Constitution, Bush is shown to be making his own judgment on who is a "bad guy."

In 2004 the U.S. Supreme Court rendered a decision consistent with Sargent's criticism. It ruled that the government could not hold the Guantánamo Bay detainees indefinitely without legal rights.

About the Cartoonist

Ben Sargent's editorial cartoons appear in nearly seventy-five newspapers across the country. He is the author of *Texas Statehouse Blues* and *Big Brother Blues*, and winner of numerous cartooning awards, including the 1982 Pulitzer Prize for editorial cartooning.

Sargent. © 2002 by Universal Press Syndicate. Reproduced by permission.

Examining Cartoon 6:
"Death to America!"

About the Cartoon

The U.S. Constitution guarantees the right to due process for anyone charged with a crime. In this cartoon, however, Mike Peters points out the irony of this right in the case of suspected terrorists. In the first panel Peters depicts an angry terrorist holding a dirty bomb, a weapon that combines radioactive material with conventional explosives and is designed to inflict a large number of casualties. His drawing implies that many terrorists hate America and are making plans to kill Americans with weapons such as dirty bombs. In the second panel, Peters suggests that only when this terrorist is caught and imprisoned for his actions does he care about constitutional rights. With these contrasting panels Peters exposes the contradiction posed by people who hate America yet demand the fair treatment that the American system guarantees.

Peters is likely alluding to the case of alleged al Qaeda terrorist José Padilla, who was arrested in 2002 in connection with the construction of a dirty bomb. Since then Padilla has been held without charges in a South Carolina prison. As of this writing, his case is still being debated in the courts.

About the Cartoonist

Dayton (Ohio) Daily News cartoonist Mike Peters' cartoons appear in numerous newspapers and magazines, including *Newsweek*, *Time*, *U.S. News & World Report*, and the *New Republic*. He has also appeared on television shows such as *Good Morning America* and *The Today Show*. In 1981 Peters was awarded a Pulitzer Prize for journalism. His political cartoon books include *The Nixon Chronicles*, *Clones*, *The Gang of Eight*, *On the Brink*, and *Happy Days Are Here Again*.

Peters. © 2002 by Tribune Media Services, Inc. Reproduced by permission.

Chapter 3

Civil Liberties and the War in Iraq

EXAMINING ISSUES THROUGH POLITICAL CARTOONS

Preface

In 1996 Iraqi citizen Falah Abdulrahman Mohamad Salih acquired a small satellite dish for his television. Under then-president Saddam Hussein satellite dishes were banned, so Salih tried to hide the dish between some laundry lines. He was unsuccessful. A few days later security police came to his door at 4 A.M. and hauled him off to prison where he spent the next six months. Under Hussein, media content in Iraq was strictly regulated. Satellite dishes were illegal because they made it possible to receive unapproved programming from countries outside Iraq. When a U.S.-led coalition invaded Iraq in 2003, they stressed that with Hussein gone, Iraqis would now enjoy media freedom. However, the coalition has faced fierce resistance to its occupation, and there are charges that, like Hussein, it has also censored the media in an attempt to maintain control of the population.

Under Hussein Iraq experienced decades-long media control by the Ministry of Information. According to journalist Illene Prushar, Hussein's eldest son, Uday, owned eleven newspapers as well as television and radio stations. "The papers always ran pictures of his father on the front cover, sometimes the same one day after day," says Prushar. She quotes Iraqi Sabah eh-Din: "If we turned on the television in the past, the only news was what Saddam did today," he says. "It would have been better to turn the television off and just paste up a picture of Saddam on the screen." Mar Ghareb, head of the media department for Kirkuk in northen Iraq echoes this opinion. "The [Kirkuk] paper . . . boasted how the government was doing good services for the people of Kirkuk and how everything was going well," says Ghareb. "They did it so people would get an inaccurate picture."

With the U.S.-led occupation in 2003 came pronouncements that these days of media censorship were over. In late 2003 George W. Bush maintained that "since the liberation of Iraq, we have seen changes that could hardly have been imagined a year ago. . . . More than 150 Iraqi newspapers are now in circulation, printing what they choose, not what they're ordered." On its Web site the White House posted "100 Days of Progress in Iraq," a document detailing the new freedoms enjoyed there. According to the document, "150 newspapers on the streets of Baghdad help get out the news of a free Iraq. . . . Says a newspaper editor: 'We can't train staff fast enough. People are desperate here for a neutral free press after 30 years of a totalitarian state.'" Prushar has visited Iraq and believes that significant progress has been made toward a free media there. In her opinion, "the sprouting of media outlets virtually overnight is remarkable." Ghareb echoes Prushar, asserting, "I'm sure that freedom is here to stay."

However, not everyone believes that the United States has brought media freedom to Iraq. There have been numerous accusations that the Iraqi media is still heavily censored, this time to facilitate the U.S. presence there. For example, in 2004 Arabic television network Al Jazeera's Baghdad office was shut down. Officials charged it with fueling anticoalition hostilities. In a statement posted on its Web site, Reporters Without Borders, a Paris-based organization that monitors media censorship worldwide, states, "We are extremely concerned about persistent episodes of [media] censorship in Iraq." Journalist Alex Gourevitch argues that censorship under Hussein has been replaced with censorship by the United States. He criticizes a 2003 statement by Paul Bremer, former envoy to Iraq. Reflecting on the new freedoms in Iraq, Bremer told journalists that they are no longer constrained by the government and are now "free to criticize whoever, or whatever, you want." In reality, says Gourevitch, that freedom does not include the ability to criticize the United States.

Media freedom is only one of the civil liberties in Iraq that has been impacted by the war there. In this chapter the cartoonists offer their views on other civil liberties in Iraq. There is no question that civil liberties were greatly restricted under Hussein. Whether or not the situation has improved is the topic of much debate.

Examining Cartoon 1:
"More Shocking Photos"

About the Cartoon

In 2004 many people were horrified by the emergence of photographs depicting U.S. soldiers abusing Iraqi prisoners at Abu Ghraib prison in Iraq. There were accusations that American actions were similar to those of former Iraqi leader Saddam Hussein, who tortured and killed thousands of his own citizens. In this cartoon, Mike Shelton suggests that these accusations are far from true. His drawing shows the media focusing on the U.S. abuses and characterizing them as "shocking." However in the background, ignored by the media, lies "Saddam's Killing Field," which contains the bones from the countless people that died under his regime. The bones stretch to the edge of the cartoon, suggesting that vast numbers of people died under Hussein's rule. By comparing these bones with the handful of photos held by the media, Shelton suggests that accusations of U.S. mistreatment are greatly exaggerated. He seems to be attempting to remind readers that while the Abu Ghraib scandal is regrettable, it is a relatively minor crime, that cannot be compared to Hussein's horrific abuses.

About the Cartoonist

Mike Shelton is editorial cartoonist for the *Orange County Register* in California. He produces cartoons on topics that range from local and national politics to international issues.

Shelton. © 2004 by King Features Syndicate. Reproduced by permission of North America Syndicate.

Examining Cartoon 2:
"Nicely Done!"

About the Cartoon

The notorious Abu Ghraib prison in Iraq was the site of the torture and execution of hundreds of political dissidents under former Iraqi ruler Saddam Hussein. The United States and other nations publicly decried Hussein's use of torture and his human rights abuses. When a U.S.-led coalition invaded Iraq in 2003, the prison became the Baghdad Correctional Facility, and the U.S. military used it to detain alleged criminals and rebels. However, in 2004 reports revealed that Abu Ghraib prisoners were again being abused and tortured, this time by U.S. soldiers.

In this cartoon Rob Rogers depicts Uncle Sam reading newspaper reports of the abuse while Hussein tells him, "Nicely Done!"

Rogers suggests that Hussein would approve of America's treatment of the Abu Ghraib prisoners. In Rogers' drawing, Uncle Sam looks into a mirror and sees himself reflected as Hussein. One of the U.S. justifications for invading Iraq was to end the human rights abuses committed there by Hussein. However, in this cartoon Rogers implies that the United States has not fulfilled its promises. By insinuating that Hussein and Uncle Sam are mirror images of one another, he suggests that America's actions in Iraq are no better than Hussein's.

About the Cartoonist

Rob Rogers is a syndicated cartoonist with United Feature Syndicate, and his cartoons appear regularly in the *New York Times*, *Washington Post*, *Philadelphia Inquirer*, *Newsweek*, and *USA Today*. He received the 1995 National Headliner Award, the 2000 Overseas Press Club Award, and seven Golden Quill Awards. In 1999 he was a finalist for the Pulitzer Prize.

Rogers. © 2004 by United Feature Syndicate, Inc. All rights reserved. Reproduced by permission.

Examining Cartoon 3:

"Another Sign of American Arrogance"

About the Cartoon

In 2004 the Arab world was outraged at photos depicting U.S. abuse of Arab prisoners at Abu Ghraib prison in Iraq. While the United States had declared its intent to bring freedom and democracy to Iraq and the rest of the Middle East, many Arabs charged that the Abu Ghraib scandal revealed America's hypocrisy. In the opinion of many the photos confirmed their view that, despite its declarations, America actually treats Arabs with prejudice and an attitude of superiority, and is concerned not with freedom and democracy but with furthering its own interests.

This cartoon by David Horsey replies to such criticism of the United States. In the first panel, Horsey presents the Arab argument by depicting a soldier who is saying, "It's another sign of American arrogance that they would torture and humiliate Arabs." However in the second panel, Horsey reveals that the soldier actually represents Arab regimes, and he is torturing one of his own people. The author seems to be suggesting that Arab criticisms of U.S. actions are hypocritical and that if anyone should be criticized, it is the Arabs themselves since they commit the majority of Arab human rights abuses.

About the Cartoonist

David Horsey, the *Seattle Post-Intelligencer* editorial cartoonist, has won two Pulitzer Prizes in journalism for editorial cartooning; one in 1998 and another in 2002.

Horsey. © 2004 by the *Seattle Post-Intelligencer*. Reproduced by permission.

Examining Cartoon 4:
"Planning for a Free Iraq"

About the Cartoon

One of the justifications the U.S. administration presented for its 2003 invasion of Iraq was that it was ending years of civil liberties abuses and bringing freedom to the people there. In this cartoon Joel Pett seems to be suggesting that in reality, American actions will not increase civil liberties in Iraq. The cartoon shows four members of the U.S. administration during the Iraq war: secretary of defense Ronald Rumsfeld, vice president Dick Cheney, former attorney general John Ashcroft, and former secretary of education Rod Paige. While the title of the cartoon says that these men are "planning for a free Iraq," Pett implies that the administration's definition of free-dom is that Iraq will be restructured according to U.S. preferences. He suggests that the United States will censor freedoms of speech, the press, and religion, and manipulate the economy in Iraq, in effect replacing the dictatorship of Saddam Hussein with an American one.

About the Cartoonist

Joel Pett, winner of the 2000 Pulitzer Prize for his editorial car-toons, has been the editorial cartoonist at the *Lexington Herald-Leader* in Kentucky since 1984. His cartoons have appeared in hundreds of newspapers and magazines nationwide, including the *New York Times*, *Washington Post*, and *Los Angeles Times*. Pett is also the 1995 winner of the Global Media Award for cartoons on popu-lation issues and has served as president of the Association of Amer-ican Editorial Cartoonists.

Pett. © 2003 by Joel Pett. Reproduced by permission.

Organizations to Contact

The editors have compiled the following list of organizations concerned with the issues debated in this book. The descriptions are derived from materials provided by the organizations. All have publications or information available for interested readers. The list was compiled at the time of publication of the present volume; the information provided here may change. Be aware that many organizations take several weeks or longer to respond to inquiries, so allow as much time as possible.

American Civil Liberties Union (ACLU)
125 Broad St., 18th Fl., New York, NY 10004
(212) 549-2500 • fax: (212) 549-2646
e-mail: aclu@aclu.org • Web site: www.aclu.org

The ACLU is a national organization that defends Americans' civil liberties guaranteed in the U.S. Constitution. It adamantly opposes the restriction of civil liberties for any reason. The ACLU offers numerous reports, fact sheets, and policy statements on a wide variety of issues. Publications include the briefing papers "America's Disappeared: Seeking International Justice for Immigrants Detained After September 11" and "Sanctioned Bias: Racial Profiling Since 9/11."

American Library Association (ALA)
50 E. Huron St., Chicago, IL 60611
(800) 545-2433 • fax: (312) 440-9347
e-mail: ala@ala.org • Web site: www.ala.org

The ALA is the nation's primary professional organization for librarians. It is opposed to the Patriot Act on the grounds that the act restricts freedom of expression in the United States. Publications of the ALA include the *Newsletter on Intellectual Freedom*, articles, fact sheets, and policy statements, including "Protecting the Freedom to Read."

Arab American Institute (AAI)
1600 K St. NW, Suite 601, Washington, DC 20006
(202) 429-9210 • Web site: www.aaiusa.org

The AAI is a nonprofit organization committed to the civic and political empowerment of Americans of Arab descent. The institute opposes ethnic profiling and the restriction of immigrants' civil liberties in the name of homeland security. It provides policy, research, and public affairs services to support a broad range of community activities. It publishes a quarterly newsletter called *Issues*, a weekly bulletin called *Countdown*, and the report *Healing the Nation: The Arab American Experience After September 11*.

The Brookings Institution
1775 Massachusetts Ave. NW, Washington, DC 20036
(202) 797-6000 • fax: (202) 797-6004
e-mail: brookinfo@brook.edu • Web site: www.brookings.org

The institution, founded in 1927, is a think tank that conducts research and education in foreign policy, economics, government, and the social sciences. Its publications include the quarterly *Brookings Review*, periodic *Policy Briefs*, and books, including *Protecting the American Homeland*. Articles, commentary, and speeches on civil liberties in the war on terror, including "Rights, Liberties, and Security: Recalibrating the Balance After September 11" and "The Rule of Law and Terrorism: The Critical Implications of a New National Debate," can be accessed using its Web site's search engine.

Canadian Association for Free Expression (CAFE)
PO Box 332, Station B, Etobicoke, ON M9W 5L3 Canada
(905) 897-7221 • e-mail: cafe@canadafirst.net
Web site: www.canadianfreespeech.com

CAFE, one of Canada's leading civil liberties groups, works to strengthen the freedom of speech and freedom of expression provisions of the Canadian Charter of Rights and Freedoms. It lobbies politicians and researches threats to the freedom of speech. Publications include specialized reports, leaflets, and the *Free Speech Monitor*, which is published ten times per year.

Cato Institute
1000 Massachusetts Ave. NW, Washington, DC 20001
(202) 842-0200 • fax (202) 842-3490
e-mail: cato@cato.org • Web site: http://www.cato.org

The Cato Institute is a libertarian public policy research foundation dedicated to limiting the role of government and promoting individual liberty. The institute publishes the quarterly magazine *Regulation*, the bimonthly *Cato Policy Report*, and numerous papers dealing with civil liberties, including "The End of the Right to Remain Silent" and "Upholding Liberty in America."

Center for Constitutional Rights (CCR)
666 Broadway, 7th Fl., New York, NY 10012
(212) 614-6464 • fax: (212) 614-6499
Web site: www.ccr-ny.org

CCR is a nonprofit legal and educational organization dedicated to protecting and advancing the rights guaranteed by the U.S. Constitution and the Universal Declaration of Human Rights. The organization uses litigation to empower minority and poor communities and to strengthen the broader movement for constitutional and human rights. It opposes the government's restriction of civil liberties since the September 11, 2001, terrorist attacks. CCR publishes books, pamphlets, fact sheets, and reports such as *The State of Civil Liberties: One Year Later*.

Central Intelligence Agency (CIA)
Office of Public Affairs, Washington, DC 20505
(703) 482-0623 • fax: (703) 482-1739
Web site: www.cia.gov

The CIA is charged with coordinating the nation's intelligence activities and correlating, evaluating, and disseminating intelligence that affects national security. The CIA is an independent agency, responsible to the president and accountable to the American people through the Intelligence Oversight Committee of the U.S. Congress. Publications, including *Factbook on Intelligence*, are available on its Web site.

Federal Bureau of Investigation (FBI)
935 Pennsylvania Ave. NW, Rm. 7972, Washington, DC 20535
(202) 324-3000 • Web site: www.fbi.gov

The FBI is the principal investigative arm of the U.S. Department of Justice. It also is authorized to provide other law enforcement agencies with cooperative services, such as fingerprint identification, laboratory examinations, and police training. The mission of the FBI includes protecting the United States from foreign intelligence and terrorist activities. Press releases, congressional statements, and major speeches on issues concerning the FBI are available on the agency's Web site.

Freedom Forum
1101 Wilson Blvd., Arlington, VA 22209
(703) 528-0800 • fax: (703) 284-2836
e-mail: news@freedomforum.org
Web site: www.freedomforum.org

The Freedom Forum is an international organization that works to protect freedom of the press and free speech. It monitors developments in media and First Amendment issues on its Web site, in its monthly magazine *Forum News*, and in the *Media Studies Journal*, published twice a year.

The Heritage Foundation

214 Massachusetts Ave. NE, Washington, DC 20002-4999
(202) 546-4400 • fax: (202) 544-8328
e-mail: info@heritage.org • Web site: www.heritage.org

The Heritage Foundation is a conservative public policy organization dedicated to free-market principles, individual liberty, and limited government. It favors limiting freedom of the press when that freedom threatens national security. Its resident scholars publish position papers on a wide variety of issues through publications such as the weekly *Backgrounder* and the quarterly *Policy Review*.

Human Rights Watch

350 Fifth Ave., 34th Fl., New York, NY 10118-3299
(212) 290-4700 • fax: (212) 736-1300
e-mail: hrwnyc@hrw.org • Web site: www.hrw.org

Human Rights Watch regularly investigates human rights abuses in over seventy countries around the world. It promotes civil liberties and defends freedom of thought, due process, and equal protection of the law. Its goal is to hold governments accountable for human rights violations they may commit against individuals because of the individuals' political, ethnic, or religious affiliations. It publishes the *Human Rights Watch Quarterly Newsletter* and the annual *Human Rights Watch World Report*.

International Freedom of Expression Exchange (IFEX)

IFEX Clearing House
489 College St., Suite 403, Toronto, ON M6G 1A5 Canada
(416) 515-9622 • fax: (416) 515-7879
e-mail: ifex@ifex.org • Web site: www.ifex.org

IFEX consists of more than forty organizations that support freedom of expression. Its work is coordinated by its Toronto-based Clearing House. Through the Action Alert Network, organizations report abuses of free expression to the Clearing House, which distributes the information throughout the world. Publications include the weekly *Communiqué*, which reports on free expression triumphs and violations.

National Coalition Against Censorship (NCAC)
275 Seventh Ave., New York, NY 10001
(212) 807-6222 • fax: (212) 807-6245
e-mail: ncac@ncac.org • Web site: www.ncac.org

The NCAC represents more than forty national organizations that work to prevent suppression of free speech and the press. It educates the public about the dangers of censorship and how to oppose it. The coalition publishes *Censorship News* five times a year, articles, various reports, and background papers.

People for the American Way (PFAW)
2000 M St. NW, Suite 400, Washington, DC 20036
(202) 467-4999 • fax: (202) 293-2672
e-mail: pfaw@pfaw.org • Web site: www.pfaw.org

PFAW works to promote citizen participation in democracy and to safeguard the principles of the U.S. Constitution, including the right to free speech. It publishes a variety of fact sheets, articles, and position statements on its Web site and distributes the e-mail newsletter *Freedom to Learn Online*.

United States Department of Justice (DOJ)
950 Pennsylvania Ave. NW, Washington, DC 20530-0001
(202) 514-2000 • e-mail: askdoj@usdoj.gov
Web site: www.usdoj.gov

The function of the DOJ is to enforce the law and defend the interests of the United States according to the law; to ensure public safety against foreign and domestic threats; to provide federal leadership in preventing and controlling crime; to seek just punishment for those guilty of unlawful behavior; to administer and enforce the nation's immigration laws fairly and effectively; and to ensure fair and impartial administration of justice for all Americans. On its Web site, the DOJ provides a link to the Web site Preserving Life & Liberty, launched to educate Americans about how the department is preserving life and liberty by using the Patriot Act. Also published on its Web site is "Report from the Field: The USA Patriot Act at Work."

For Further Research

Books

Randall P. Bezanson, *How Free Can the Press Be?* Urbana: University of Illinois Press, 2003.

Cynthia Brown, *Lost Liberties: Ashcroft and the Assault on Personal Freedom.* New York: New Press, 2003.

Elaine Cassel, *The War on Civil Liberties: How Bush and Ashcroft Have Dismantled the Bill of Rights.* Westport, CT: Lawrence Hill, 2004.

David B. Cohen and John B. Wells, eds., *American National Security and Civil Liberties in an Era of Terrorism.* New York: Palgrave Macmillan, 2004.

David Cole, James X. Dempsey, and Carole Goldberg, *Terrorism and the Constitution: Sacrificing Civil Liberties in the Name of National Security.* New York: New Press, 2005.

Katherine B. Darmer, Robert M. Baird, and Stuart E. Rosenbaum, *Civil Liberties vs. National Security in a Post 9/11 World.* Amherst, NY: Prometheus, 2004.

Richard Delgado, *Justice at War.* New York: New York University Press, 2003.

Alan Dershowitz, *Shouting Fire: Civil Liberties in a Turbulent Age.* Boston: Little, Brown, 2002.

Danny Goldberg, Robert Greenwald, and Victor Goldberg, *It's a Free Country: Personal Freedom in America After September 11.* Brooklyn, NY: Akashic, 2002.

Catherine Embree Harris, *Dusty Exile: Looking Back at Japanese Relocation During World War II*. Honolulu: Mutual, 1999.

Richard C. Leone and Greg Anrig Jr., eds., *The War on Our Freedoms: Civil Liberties in an Age of Terrorism*. New York: PublicAffairs, 2003.

Michael Linfield, *Freedom Under Fire: U.S. Civil Liberties in Times of War*. Boston: South End, 1990.

Mike Mackey, ed., *Guilt by Association: Essays on Japanese Settlement, Internment, and Relocation in the Rocky Mountain West*. Powell, WY: Western History Publications, 2001.

Michael Moore, *Dude, Where's My Country?* New York: Warner, 2003.

William H. Rehnquist, *All the Laws but One*. New York: Alfred A. Knopf, 1998.

Mark Sidel, *More Secure, Less Free? Antiterrorism Policy and Civil Liberties after September 11*. Ann Arbor: University of Michigan Press, 2004.

Harold J. Sullivan, *Civil Rights and Liberties: Provocative Questions and Evolving Answers*. Upper Saddle River, NJ: Prentice-Hall, 2001.

John Tateishi, *And Justice for All: An Oral History of the Japanese American Detention Camps*. Seattle: University of Washington Press, 1984.

Periodicals

Bob Barr, "Patriot Act Games: It Can Happen Here," *American Spectator*, August/September 2003.

———, "Patriot Fixes," *Wall Street Journal*, November 12, 2004.

Peter Berkowitz, "Two Out of Three Ain't Bad," *Weekly Standard*, July 19, 2004.

Matt Bowles, "The State, Power, and Resistance: Organizing for Our Civil Liberties," *Left Turn*, May/June 2003.

Elaine Cassel, "Civil Liberties: Where Do We Stand?" *Left Turn*, March/April 2004.

Erwin Chemerinsky, "Giving Up Our Rights for Little Gain," *Los Angeles Times*, September 27, 2001.

Richard Cohen, "It's Not the American Way," *Liberal Opinion Week*, June 14, 2004.

David Cole, "Operation Enduring Liberty," *Nation*, June 3, 2002.

———, "Outlaws on Torture," *Nation*, June 28, 2004.

Mark Engler, "Homeland Security for Whom?" *Z Magazine*, September 2003.

Amitai Etzioni, "Better Safe than Sorry," *Weekly Standard*, July 21, 2003.

Nat Hentoff, "War on the Bill of Rights," *In These Times*, September 29, 2003.

Robert Higgs, "It Just Ain't So!" *Ideas on Liberty*, March 2002.

Michael Ignatieff, "Lesser Evils," *New York Times Magazine*, May 2, 2004.

Jeff Jacoby, "Overblown Fears About the Patriot Act," *Conservative Chronicle*, May 23, 2004.

William F. Jasper, "Trading Freedom for Security," *New American*, May 5, 2003.

Kenneth Jost, "Civil Liberties Debates: Are Rights Being Lost in the War on Terrorism?" *CQ Researcher*, October 24, 2003.

Wendy Kaminer, "Back to the Future," *Free Inquiry*, June/July 2004.

Charles Levendosky, "Congress Acts to Curb Police Powers," *Progressive Populist*, September 1, 2003.

Robert Lovato, "Big Liberty Is Watching," *In These Times*, July 21, 2003.

Timothy Lynch, "Hamdi and Habeas Corpus," *Wall Street Journal*, April 28, 2004.

Kate Martin, "Intelligence, Terrorism, and Civil Liberties," *Human Rights*, Winter 2002.

Michael McClintock, "The Trials of Liberty," *Index for Free Expression*, July 2003.

Richard A. Posner, "The Truth About Our Liberties," *Responsive Community*, Summer 2002.

Thomas F. Powers, "The End of Gitmo Limbo," *Weekly Standard*, September 27, 2004.

———, "When to Hold 'Em," *Legal Affairs*, September/October 2004.

Christy Reilly, "Warning! You Are Being Watched," *In These Times*, October 13, 2003.

Tom Teepen, "Fundamental Freedoms on Trial," *Liberal Opinion Week*, January 5, 2004.

Laurence H. Tribe, "We Can Strike a Balance on Civil Liberties," *Wall Street Journal*, September 27, 2001.

Jonathan Turley, "Liberty Ebbs by Degrees," *Liberal Opinion Week*, January 13, 2003.

Lynne A. Williams, "Rights at Risk," *Towards Freedom*, Spring 2004.

Patricia J. Williams, "To See or Not to See," *Nation*, June 28, 2004.

Index

Fluvanna County High School
Library Media Center
3717 Central Plains Rd.
Palmyra, VA 22963

DATE DUE

FOLLETT